D1799793

14 N

30

REDBORNE SCHOOL
REDBORNE
LIBRARY
AMPTHILL

# JUST LOOK AT...
# CLOTHES

## Brenda Ralph Lewis

Macdonald Educational

014214

**Factual Adviser:** Avril Lansdell
(Weybridge Museum, Surrey)

**Editor:** Valerie Hunt-Taylor
**Teacher Panel:** Tim Firth,
Bernadette Hill, Ann Merriman
**Designer:** Ewing Paddock
**Picture Research:** Kathy Lockley
**Production:** Rosemary Bishop

Illustrations
Anna Hancock 8-9, 10-11, 12T, 16-17, 18-19
20-21, 24-25, 27, 29, 31, 33, 34-35, 38
Maggie Raynor 19T, 22, 26, 41, back cover
Julian Baker/Maltings Partnership 12B

Photographs
Aldus Archive: 43TL, 43MR
All-Sport: 26
Barnaby's: 41
Bridgeman Art Library: 43M
Bristol Art Gallery: 14–15
BBC Hulton Picture Library: 20
Courtaulds Clothing Ltd: 12
Zoe Dominic Photography: 32
Fitzwilliam Museum, Cambridge: 40L
Robert Harding Picture Library: Title page, 19,
28BL
Valerie Hunt-Taylor: 42
I.B.M.: 25
H.R. Lewis: 11
NOW: 36
Photo Source: 28–9M
Pictorial Press: 39L
Popperfoto: 30, 39R
Rex Features: 33, 36–7
Spectrum Colour Library: 17, 31
Frank Spooner Pictures: Cover
Sporting Pictures (UK) Ltd: 22–3, 35
Wessex Photography: 24
ZEFA: 14BL, 40R

Title page photo: A Lapp family in Norway wearing
their colourful traditional clothes.

British Library Cataloguing in Publication Data
Lewis, Brenda Ralph
    Clothes. – (Just look at)
    I. Clothing and dress – Juvenile literature
    I. Title    II. Series
    646'.3    GT518
    ISBN 0-356-11478-3

## How to use this book
Look first in the contents page to see if the subject you want is listed. For instance, if you want to find out about sports clothes, you will find that they are on pages 34 and 35. The word list explains the more difficult terms found in this book. The index will tell you how many times a particular subject is mentioned and whether there is a picture of it.

**Clothes** is one of a series of books on Our World. All the books on this subject have a blue colour band around the cover. If you want to know more about the world around us and our bodies, look for other books with a blue band in the **Just Look At . . . series.**

© Macdonald & Co. (Publishers) Ltd. 1986

First published in Great Britain in 1986
by Macdonald & Co. (Publishers) Ltd.
London & Sydney

Printed and bound in Great Britain by Purnell
Book Production Ltd., Paulton, nr. Bristol.

Macdonald & Co. (Publishers) Ltd.
Greater London House, Hampstead Road,
London NW1 7QX.

Members of BPCC plc. *All rights reserved.*

# CONTENTS

# WHY CLOTHES?

One of the first things most people do after they get up in the morning is to put on their clothes. However, these clothes will be different, depending, for instance, on the sort of work they do or the kind of climate in which they live.

It is very cold in winter in northern Europe, Central Asia, Canada, Russia and high mountain regions such as the Himalayas, in Asia. So here, people put on thicker clothes, or they wear several layers of clothing: this way, air gets trapped between the layers and this helps to keep people warm.

In hot places, like India or Africa, people wear light clothes made of thin materials. Often, these clothes are loose and flowing. They let air circulate about the body, and in this way they help people to keep cool.

Some people wear special clothes, usually because of the work they do. Factory workers, for instance, may need clothes to protect them from dust, heat or dangerous chemicals. Others wear uniforms as part of their daily work. Members of the police wear uniforms. So do soldiers and sailors and people who work for airlines, shipping lines or the railways.

Different kinds of styles of clothes are worn by men and women all over the world, and there are many interesting reasons why people dress the way they do. However, there is one thing which everyone has in common. Of the world's living creatures, land animals have fur or thick hides. Birds have feathers. Sea creatures have scales, shells or fatty skins. But only human beings wear clothes.

At different times and in different places, people have worn many different styles of clothes. These pages show you some of the ways in which people have dressed.

# About Materials

Clothes have always been made from materials which people found in the world about them.

## Furs
Long ago, prehistoric people scraped and cleaned the skins of animals they killed for food, and wore them as clothes. They thought this gave them the animals' bravery and strength. Even today, people wear animal skins, usually to keep themselves warm. Furs are also worn as fashion clothes, though some people think it wrong to kill animals for this purpose. Nowadays, in places like Russia and the Arctic, many people wear synthetic materials rather than furs as protection from the icy climate.

## Clothes from plants
Plants can be used to make clothes. Large leaves may be worn as skirts. Grass may be woven or knotted into robes. Six or seven centuries ago, in Britain, a linen-like cloth was made from the stalks of stinging nettles.

## Cotton and flax
Cotton and flax (for linen) are also natural fibres from plants, but the plants do not grow wild in woods or meadows. Farmers grow them as crops in fields, where they are easily harvested.

In about 3000 BC Indians in the Indus Valley grew cotton. Later, the idea of growing cotton spread to Egypt and the Nile Valley and to other parts of Africa. Much later, the growing of cotton spread to America and the rest of the world.

## Wool
Animals can also be used to 'grow' materials for clothing. For thousands of years farmers have kept flocks of sheep and sheared (cut) their thick fleeces (coats) to make wool. In Peru and Bolivia, thousands of metres high up in the Andes mountains of South America, the Incas used to keep flocks of llamas, alpacas and vicunas. Warm ponchos (short cloaks) are still made from the wool of these animals.

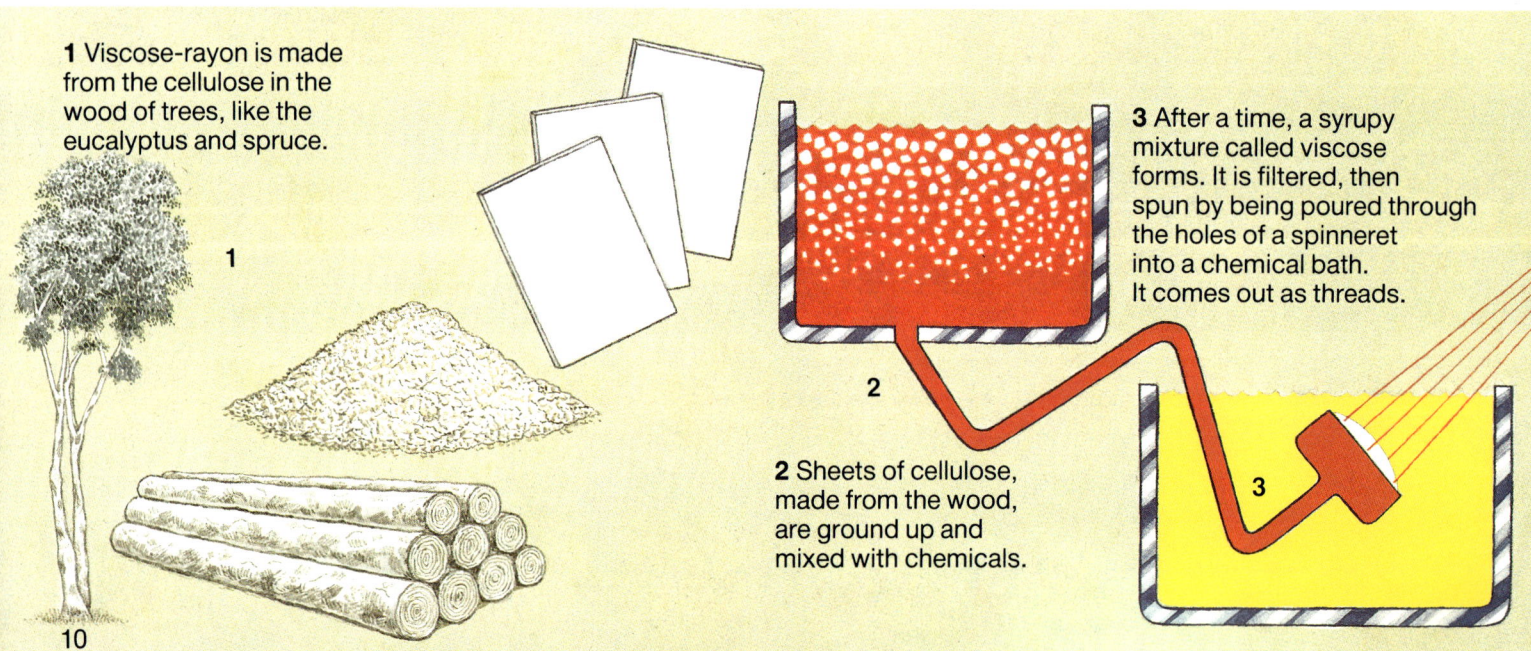

**1** Viscose-rayon is made from the cellulose in the wood of trees, like the eucalyptus and spruce.

**3** After a time, a syrupy mixture called viscose forms. It is filtered, then spun by being poured through the holes of a spinneret into a chemical bath. It comes out as threads.

**2** Sheets of cellulose, made from the wood, are ground up and mixed with chemicals.

▲ Neanderthal people lived about 100 000 years ago. They killed animals for food and used the skins to make clothes.

▲The Yagua Indians, from the Amazon region of Peru, are one of the few peoples of the world who still wear a traditional skirt made of grasses.

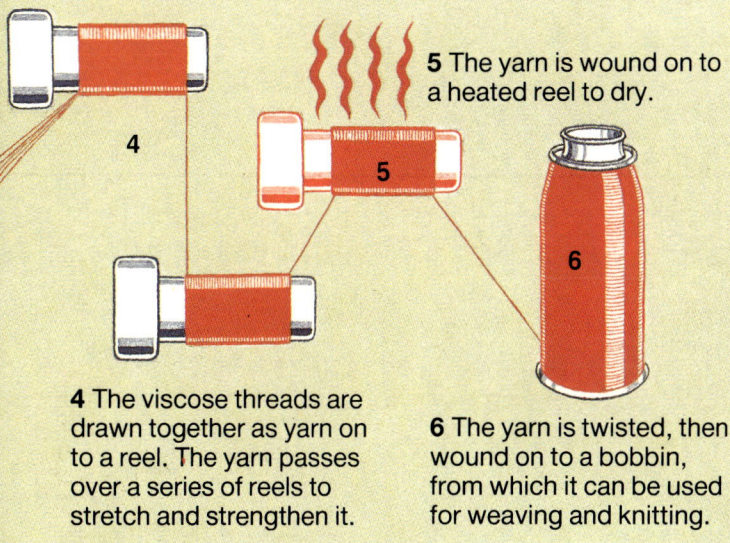

**5** The yarn is wound on to a heated reel to dry.

**4** The viscose threads are drawn together as yarn on to a reel. The yarn passes over a series of reels to stretch and strengthen it.

**6** The yarn is twisted, then wound on to a bobbin, from which it can be used for weaving and knitting.

## Silk

Another animal material, silk, was made from the cocoons of silkworm larvae. The Chinese made silk over 4000 years ago. For a long time its manufacture was secret. Anyone who gave the secret away could be punished by death. Even so, the Japanese learned about silk around AD 300. Much later, Asian merchants sold this lovely, shiny material to the Europeans.

## Artificial fibres

Artificial fibres do not grow: they are made. The first to be made was viscose-rayon, using cellulose taken from plants. Other artificial fibres, called synthetics, are made from chemical mixtures called polymers. Viscose-rayon was first made in France in 1889, but only after 1950 were viscose-rayon and other synthetics, chiefly nylon, polyester and acrylic, made in large quantities. Today, cheap artificial fibres are used to make many clothes.

# How Clothes Are Made

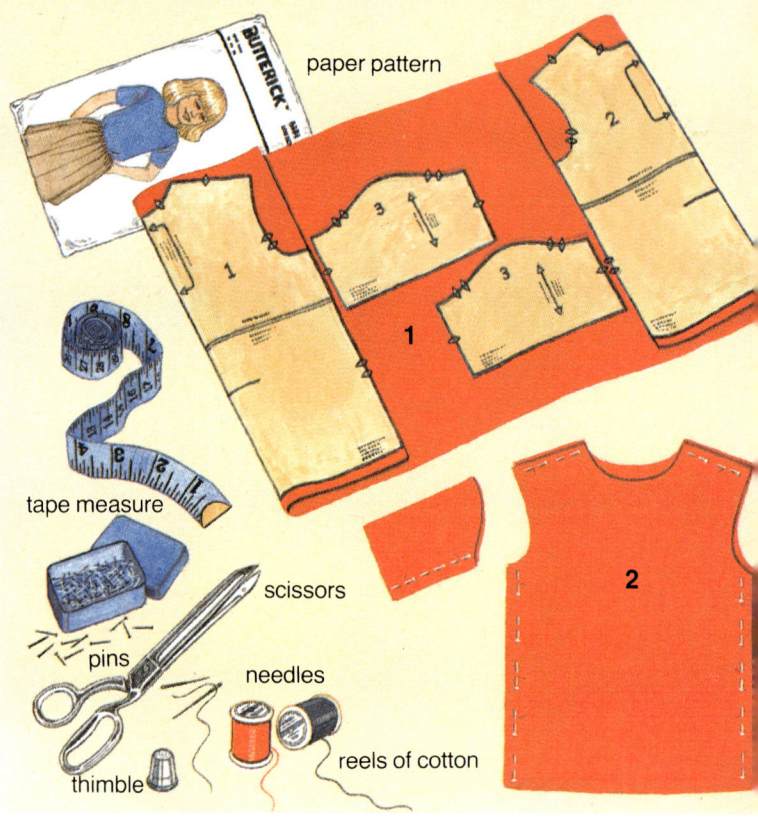

paper pattern

tape measure

scissors

pins

needles

thimble

reels of cotton

When people first wore animal skins, they tied and draped them round the body. Later, they learned to cut and sew the skins so that they were shaped and fitted the body better.

## Shaped clothes

For these shaped clothes, skins were cut with animal bone, stone or wood knives. Then the pieces were sewn together with thread made from vegetable fibre or animal sinew (muscles). Needles made from fish or animal bone were used for thousands of years. Metal needles, made of iron, were first used about 700 years ago.

For a long time, too, shaped clothes were made by hand. The cotton, linen or wool from which they were made was spun by simple hand-machines, like the distaff and spindle, or by spinning wheels. They were then woven into cloth on hand-operated looms.

## Machines

People still sew by hand today. They also knit clothes like jumpers on long needles that loop and knot thread into fabric. Today, though, machines do most clothes-making and knitting. The first knitting machine was made in 1589, in England. The first sewing machines were made, also in England, in about 1790, when the first machines to spin and weave thread were producing cloth in north of England factories.

◄ In this busy modern factory, clothes are 'mass-produced', or made in large quantities, on the most up-to-date machinery.

The latest knitting machines for use in the home have their own computer memory and can be programmed to knit a variety of stitches and patterns, using different colours and yarns. This one can even be programmed to knit from your own drawing. ►

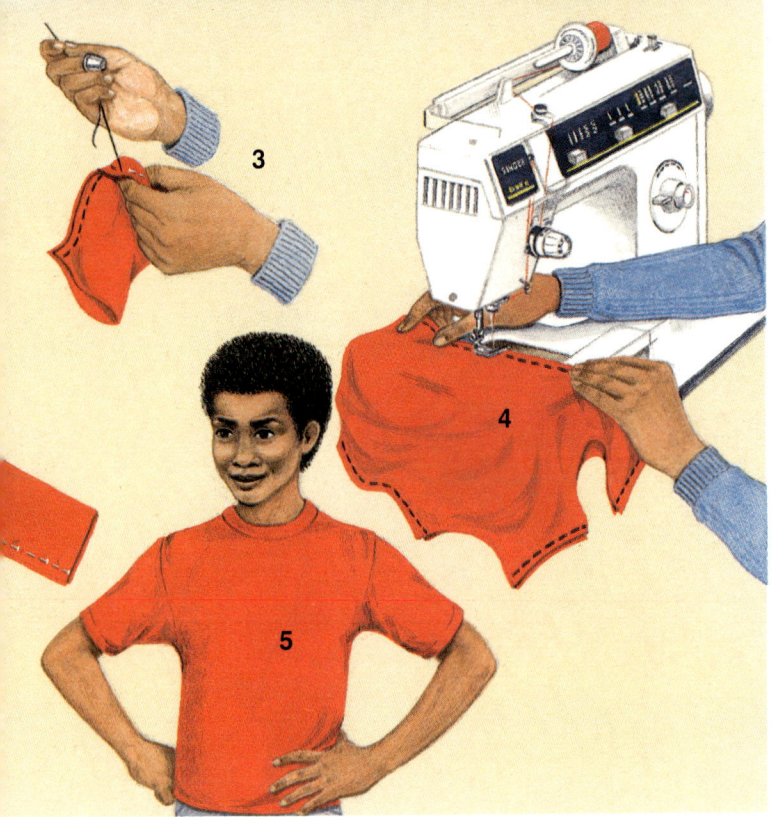

◄ The stages in making a tee-shirt:

**1** The material is cut into a front, back and two sleeves.
**2** The front, back and two sleeves are pinned together.
**3** The pieces are tacked, or loosely sewn, ready for machining.
**4** Using the sewing machine.
**5** The finished garment.

## Draped clothes

Not all clothes worn today are cut, sewn and shaped to fit. In hot countries people often prefer loosely-draped clothes. The lovely saris worn by many Indian and Sri Lankan women, for example, are just long pieces of cloth. A short-sleeved, shaped bodice reaching the ribs is worn under the sari, but the sari itself is tucked and draped into folds round the figure. Similarly, in parts of southeast Asia, like Thailand or Malaysia, many men and women wear draped ankle-length skirts called sarongs.

Sarongs and saris are as old or older than the tunics worn in Ancient Greece or the togas worn in Ancient Rome. The Greek tunic was, at first, just two pieces of cloth knotted or pinned at the shoulder. Roman togas, like saris, were basically nothing more than lengths of cloth which were draped around the body and hung in folds.

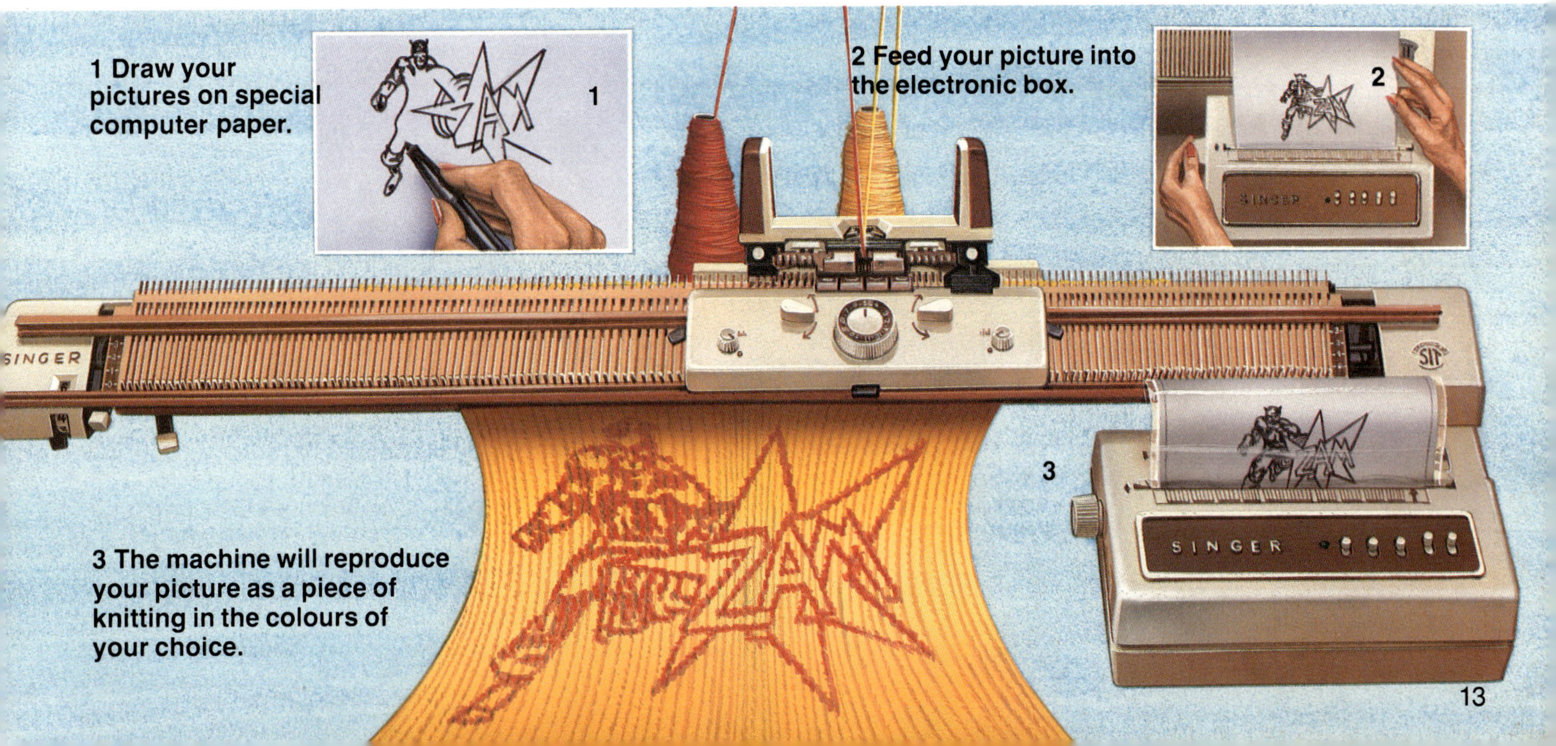

## Mass-production

Nowadays, there are machines which can cut materials to shape from patterns, stitch the material, and even make buttonholes. There are also machines for heat-sealing the seams (edges) of some synthetic materials. Because materials are made into clothes by factory machines, they can be produced in very large numbers. When clothes are made in this way, by large-scale manufacture, we call it 'mass-production'.

**1** Draw your pictures on special computer paper.

**2** Feed your picture into the electronic box.

**3** The machine will reproduce your picture as a piece of knitting in the colours of your choice.

# EVERYDAY CLOTHES

Everyday clothes are the sort we wear most often. These clothes are not the same for everyone, though. In 15th-century Europe, for example, rich and poor wore tunics as everyday clothes. However, the poor peasant's tunic was made of rough, plain cloth. By contrast, tunics worn by rich merchants or nobles were much finer and softer, and could be decorated with patterns or jewels.

Sometimes, everyday clothes have shown the importance of the people wearing them. For example, in Ancient Egypt only priests were allowed to wear linen. In Ancient Mexico the Aztec tecuhtli (nobles) showed their rank by the length of their tunics. Ordinary Aztecs who wore this length of tunic were very harshly punished.

In Europe until the 18th century, sumptuary laws told people what to wear. These laws forbade people to wear clothes or to have possessions which their rulers thought too rich or fine for them.

Today, there are no sumptuary laws, but we still have clear ideas about what is suitable everyday clothing. For example, if a businessman came to his office dressed, not in his usual smart suit, but in the jeans, sweater, Wellington boots and other clothes he wore for weekend gardening, he would look very odd and very much out of place.

The everyday clothes of the well-to-do visitors at this 18th-century country market are much finer than the plain, practical dress of the local village people. ▶

◀ Everyday dress for Bolivian market women is a wide, stiff skirt and bowler hat. Their thick skirts make it more comfortable for them to sit on the ground when they are selling their wares.

# Ancient Times

Everyday clothes were very simple in Ancient Egypt, Greece and Rome. The Egyptians lived some 4000 years ago in the hot, humid areas around the River Nile. Egyptian women usually wore long, loose shifts (dresses) made of thin materials. Men wore short skirts draped round their waists, reaching to their knees.

## Tunics and togas

In Greece the climate was often very cold. So, Greeks might dress in many layers of clothes, one on top of the other. Men and women wore tunics called 'chitons': the men's were short and reached the knees; the women's were long and reached to the ground. These chitons hung in beautiful, elegant folds.

Over their chitons, Greek women of this time wore extra robes called 'peplos'. Men wore knee-length cloaks called 'chlamys'. The 'himation' was a large, warm cloak which was worn by men and women to protect themselves in cold weather.

Romans dressed in much the same way as the Greeks, though richer, more important Romans wore long togas. Poorer Romans had to make do with short tunics, and cloaks called 'paenulae' for extra warmth in winter.

Everyday clothes in Ancient Greece and Rome were usually very plain, though sometimes they had patterned borders. The peoples who lived 4000 years ago in Crete and Persia preferred brightly coloured all-over patterns. Cretan women wore long shaped clothes. Men wore short kilts. Persian men wore fancy tunics with scalloped (rounded) edges to them. Most Persians, Cretans, Egyptians, Greeks and Romans lived in towns or cities. Here, houses could have bathrooms, heating, lighting and other comforts.

▲ The graceful toga of the clean-shaven Roman senator contrasts with the thick, rough trousers of the bearded Germanic tribesman. Both wear leather sandals and their own styles of jewellery.

Next, the sari is wound round the body, part-folded, and tucked into the petticoat.

**2**

**1**

The sari is a draped garment that has been worn in India for over 2200 years. To put it on, first, one end of the sari is tucked into a petticoat.

**3**

Finally, the loose end is spread out over the bodice and thrown over one shoulder.

An Indian man wearing the traditional dhoti. This is a piece of cloth tied to make a baggy garment.

## Trousers

However, outside the Roman Empire, Germanic and Celtic tribes lived different lives – hard, dangerous and not at all comfortable. These people lived by hunting, farming and raiding, a way of life which meant that their men had to be very skilful horseriders. For horseriding, trousers rather than Roman-style tunics were the most practical clothes to wear. All the Germanic men wore long woollen trousers. The women wore long, thick woollen skirts. In the rough settlements inside forest clearings where these people lived, only their warm clothing and a large fire gave protection from the cold.

Many Greeks and Romans considered trousers to be very rough garments. However, Roman soldiers had very different ideas. Their job was to guard the borders of the Roman Empire from invasion by the Germanic tribes. And out in the cold, wet regions far from the comforts of Rome, many soldiers began wearing trousers for warmth and convenience, just like their Germanic opponents.

The kimono (gown) and obi (sash) worn by these girls were worn by women in Japan from ancient times till this century. ▶

# Suits for Men

In cities around the world today you can see men dressed in European, or Western-style, suits – jackets, trousers, shirts and ties.

The history of men's suits goes back to the loose tunics of Ancient Greece and Rome, and the trousers worn by the Ancient Germans and Celts. After Germanic tribes raided Rome in the 5th century (which helped bring about the end of the Roman Empire) more and more Roman men began wearing loose trousers. So, for the first time, trousers became everyday clothes for men in Europe. Over the centuries that followed, trousers went through many changes.

## Hose and breeches

Knights and feudal lords going on crusades to the Holy Land after 1096 brought back eastern ideas about clothes. They began wearing oriental silks and damasks, with close-fitting hose, which were rather like women's tights. Men's hose lasted a long time, until the 17th century, when they were replaced by breeches which reached to the knees. As time went on, breeches became so wide and full that they looked like women's skirts and were known as 'petticoat breeches'. Then, in 1660, King Charles II came to the English throne, after eleven years of exile in Europe, and brought with him many new fashion ideas.

◀ In the 16th century, before the first signs of the modern suit, men dressed colourfully, displaying their legs in hose.

In the early 17th century, the doublet and breeches worn by men became longer. ▶

The late 17th century saw the first suit, with a new long coat and waistcoat, over breeches. ▶

One hundred years later, many of the frills had gone, and the waistcoat looked more like a modern one. ▶

▲ In the 19th century, it was the fashion for men to wear hats. They had different hats for every occasion.

◄ In the early 19th century, long trousers replaced breeches, and jackets began to look more like modern ones.

By the end of the 19th century, men were wearing suits very like those of today, but not quite so neat and smart. ►

## The first suit

One of these fashions was a new 'suit'. It had a long 'Persian' coat with wide turned-back sleeves and buttons down the front, worn with a long 'vest', or waistcoat, and close-fitting breeches. Royal people have always led fashion, so other men began wearing these clothes, too. They found them more practical. For the next century, men went on wearing this fashion. Then, in 1789, there was revolution in France. Men's fashions began copying the baggy trousers worn by the revolutionary people, known as 'sans culottes' ('without fine breeches'). So long trousers for men came back in fashion. Though their shape changed in the 19th century, they were now a recognizable part of today's man's suit.

While trousers were altering, tunics, now tucked into trousers, had grown sleeves and collars to become shirts. Coats and vests also changed and became closer-fitting. By 1900, they had the shape of the modern suit jacket and waistcoat.

As for men's ties, these came from the neckcloths worn by 17th-century soldiers from Croatia, in eastern Europe. Men copied these 'cravats', as the neckcloths came to be called. Cravats gradually shrank in size from the width of a scarf to the long, narrower neckties which are usually worn with a suit by men today.

# Skirts

We often think of trousers as traditional for men, and skirts as traditional for women. There is no definite rule, though. For example, in North Africa and the Middle East, Arab men as well as women wear long, loose robes called kaftans. On the other hand, in the Punjab region of eastern India, women traditionally wear long slim-fitting trousers underneath their tunics.

In Ancient Rome and the rest of Europe women continued wearing skirts after men began to wear trousers. The centuries-old loose or belted tunic for women was not replaced until after about 1400, and then by a tight-waisted, full-skirted gown. The gown went through many changes, but all of them had the long, toe-length skirt until only about 65 years ago. At times, skirts became extremely wide, supported by strange devices underneath. One was the 16th-century farthingale, a hooped frame. Another was the 19th-century crinoline, which began as a set of some twelve or more stiff petticoats.

Small boys once dressed in skirts, like girls: here is a future British king, George V, aged two, in 1867. ▼

The simple medieval (14th century) dress on the left contrasts with the fussier style shown above, worn in the 17th century.

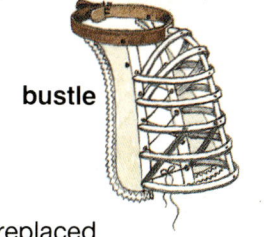

bustle

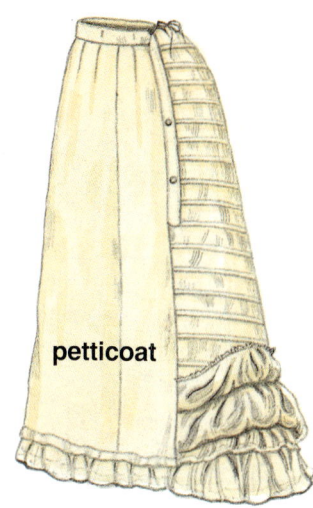

petticoat

◄ Bustles replaced crinolines under fashionable women's dress after 1870. One or more petticoats were worn over these special frames. The women who wore these elaborate styles usually employed at least one maid to help them dress.

## Cumbersome skirts

These fashions made it difficult for women to move about easily unlike men, whose trousers were more suitable for active lives. In fact, women's clothes seemed to show the way men regarded them: as not suitable to handle the responsibilities that went with owning property, voting in elections, or doing professional work as doctors or lawyers. These ideas also applied to poor women, who worked long, hard hours on farms or in factories. They, too, had to wear long skirts which often got in the way of their work.

## Freedom in clothes

In the late 19th century, though, women began to protest about all this. They wanted to feel more comfortable in their clothes, and they also wanted more independence. In the 1880s they took up bicycling, seeing in it a chance of greater freedom to travel. For this new sport, women wore 'bloomers', or loose-fitting knee breeches, which made riding bicycles easier. Some strong-minded women, known as the 'New Women', began to wear plainer, more practical clothes and refused to put on uncomfortable, restricting corsets.

However, it was not until after 1918 that women began to have more equality with men: this included the right to vote in elections. This new emancipation, or freedom, soon showed in the way women dressed. There was a complete change in clothes, particularly for younger women. Women's skirts became short for the very first time. They were so short that by 1926 they were knee-length. By the 1930s women were wearing trousers, shorts and brief swimsuits, as well as backless evening dresses. Quite apart from showing their legs in public for the first time, women were revealing more of themselves than had ever publicly been seen before.

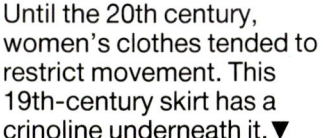

Until the 20th century, women's clothes tended to restrict movement. This 19th-century skirt has a crinoline underneath it. ▼

In the 1920s and '30s, women's clothes completely changed. The fashion was for short skirts and close-cut hair.

# SPECIAL CLOTHES

Clothes have always been more than just something for covering our bodies. Clothes have played an important part of human life and history by making certain things possible.

Identification is one of them. For example, unless a policewoman wears her special uniform you cannot know she is a policewoman. Soldiers, ballet dancers, sportspeople, religious leaders – all of them look just like everyone else without their special clothes. But *with* these clothes you know at once who they are.

Many advances, especially in science and technology, could not have been made without special clothing to protect people from surroundings which are unsuitable for them. For instance, people cannot live in the cold airlessness of space. Fish and other sea creatures can breathe in water, but we cannot. If outside temperatures fall too low, people can develop hypothermia (lowering of body heat) and this can kill them. Special clothes have solved many of these problems. This is how suitably dressed astronauts are able to travel in space, work outside their spacecraft and go out onto the surface of the cold and airless Moon. Divers can work under water, sometimes at great depths and pressures that would kill them without suits, while scientists are able to live and work in the frozen, lonely landscape of Antarctica.

American football is a rough game. Players can be hurt, so they wear protective pads on their bodies, and helmets on their heads. The body-padding has the added effect of making the players seem bigger and more powerful than they actually are. ▶

◄ On building sites, hard hats are worn to protect heads from falling objects.

HARD HAT AREA

# Clothes for Protection

The idea of using clothing for protection is a very old one. Our survival instinct has always told us to protect ourselves from harm. Nearly 3000 years ago, the Greek poet Homer wrote of a gardener who wore leather gaiters and gloves as protection from bramble-scratches. Gloves were a basic form of protection for many workers, such as shepherds out on the cold hills with their flocks, craftsmen whose hands could be damaged by splinters, or blacksmiths who used hot metals. Hand injuries could stop them from working and earning their living. Blacksmiths also wore aprons, another type of protection also used by cooks, shoemakers and other workers, and still worn today. Leather aprons shielded blacksmiths from injury should horses kick them while being shoed, or if hot sparks flew out of the forge while they were working. Hot sparks could also damage the eyes, so workers made goggles of wire gauze.

Cowboys wear 'chaps' over their trousers to protect their legs from falls or horse bites. The hat, bandana (scarf) and gloves are also protective clothes. ▶

## Protection out of doors

Farmworkers, carters, wagonners and others who worked out of doors needed all-over protection. In farming and craft trades, centuries of experience had shown people what protective clothing they needed for their work. From the 18th century onwards, they wore smocks to shield them from mud, dirt from animals or from the loads they had to carry. Smocks, together with wide hats for protection against sun and rain, were worn by male farmworkers until well into this century. So were the sun bonnets worn by women, especially at harvest time. Sun bonnets stretched down far enough to protect the back of the neck from hot sunshine because the neck was particularly likely to be burned by the sun.

## Protection underground

Miners developed their own forms of protection against falling rocks and other underground dangers, by wearing back aprons with head and neck coverings. Female, as well as male miners used to wear trousers and protected themselves against dust by covering their faces with a cloth or by wearing leather blinkers.

◀ Anyone who works with or near fire must wear protection. These fire-fighters are wearing one-piece fire-fighting suits made of a special aluminium material.

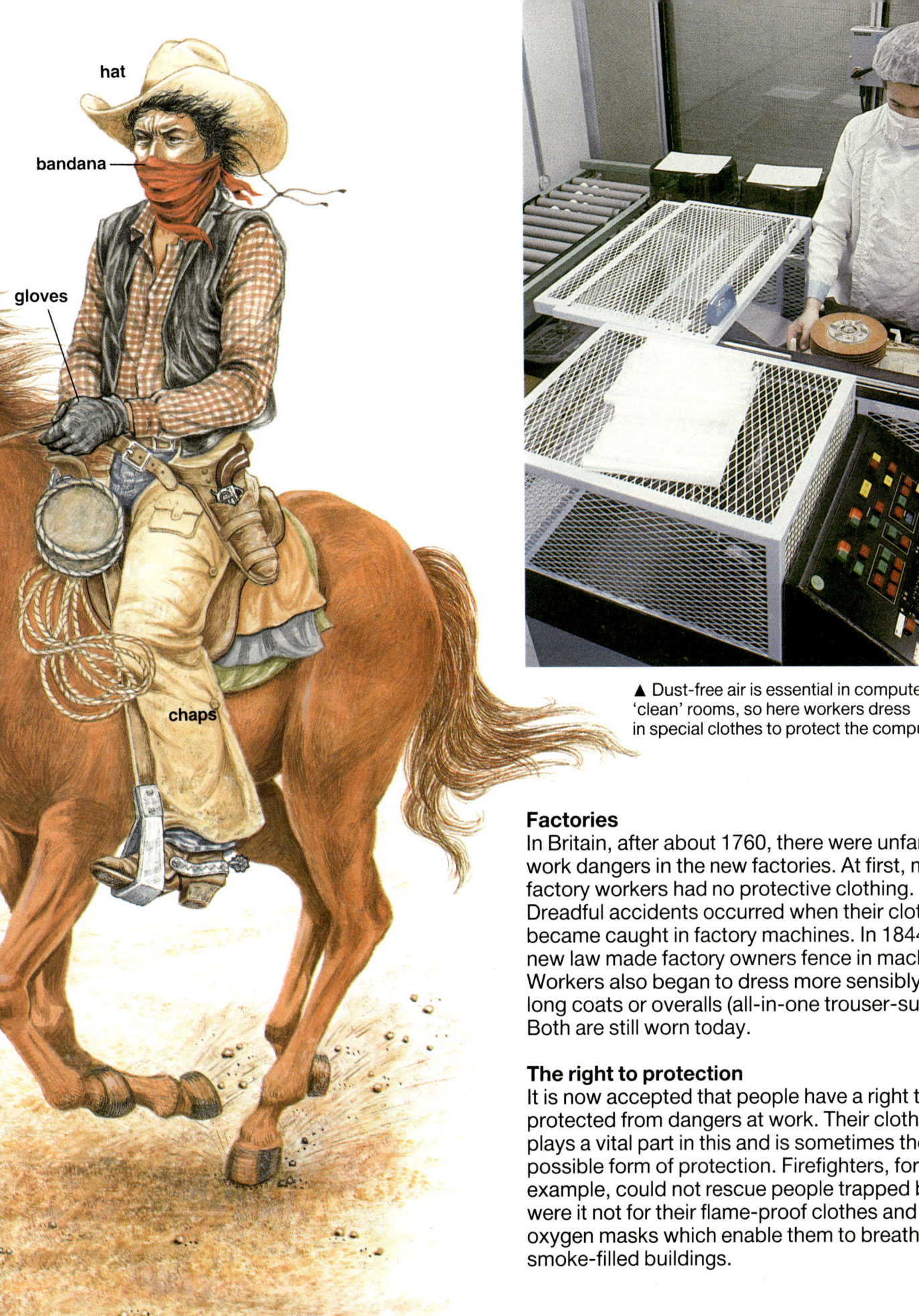

hat

bandana

gloves

chaps

▲ Dust-free air is essential in computer
'clean' rooms, so here workers dress
in special clothes to protect the computers.

## Factories

In Britain, after about 1760, there were unfamiliar
work dangers in the new factories. At first, most
factory workers had no protective clothing.
Dreadful accidents occurred when their clothes
became caught in factory machines. In 1844 a
new law made factory owners fence in machines.
Workers also began to dress more sensibly in
long coats or overalls (all-in-one trouser-suits).
Both are still worn today.

## The right to protection

It is now accepted that people have a right to be
protected from dangers at work. Their clothing
plays a vital part in this and is sometimes the only
possible form of protection. Firefighters, for
example, could not rescue people trapped by fire
were it not for their flame-proof clothes and the
oxygen masks which enable them to breathe in
smoke-filled buildings.

# Uniforms

Human beings like being together, and our lives are so arranged that we belong to groups of people. The most important group is the family, but there are others, and some of them have uniforms to show they are groups.

### Different kinds of uniform
The word uniform means 'one' or 'the same' form. Some schools like children to wear a uniform in order to show that they all go to that school, and also to show that, in school, all the children are equal. Nurses wear very practical, hygienic uniforms which are suitable for their job of caring for people who are ill. Some charity or welfare groups, like the Salvation Army or St John Ambulance Brigade, also have their own uniforms. Some clothes are uniforms because of their different colours. Football teams, for instance, wear the same kind of clothes, usually shorts and tee-shirts. But they are of different colours so that spectators at a game are able to tell one side from the other.

### Some special uniforms
Uniforms can also mark people out by having a special style. One of these special styles is the bonnet worn by women in the Salvation Army. They are like 19th-century bonnets, but today no one else wears them. In the past, servants of noble or rich families wore a special uniform called a 'livery'. Each family had its own livery, so everyone knew that the servants who wore it worked for that family and no other.

In expensive restaurants a chef wears a clean, white uniform of double-breasted jacket, tall hat and apron. The purpose of these clothes is to keep both the chef and the food clean! ▶

◀ Each team of athletes representing their country at the Olympic Games has its own uniform. These athletes come from Brazil.

An officer's parade dress in the French Foreign Legion (on the right) is severe, but smart. His 'combat-dress' (above) for going into battle is an efficient, modern design.

On parade, a Welsh Guards officer (on the right) wears a tall bearskin hat and scarlet coat. His combat clothes (above) are plain and practical, in 'camouflage' colours.

## Military uniforms

Wearing uniforms gives people a feeling of belonging or comradeship. Particularly in the armed forces, a uniform can be a type of discipline, for it can have its own special meaning and value. 'Disgracing the uniform' by bad behaviour is not a desirable thing. Soldiers in the army wear the uniforms of their particular regiment. These uniforms may carry badges and other decorations which show a regiment's history and traditions. These include victories which the regiment has won. This makes soldiers feel that they share the glories of the regiment with those who fought for them in the past; a regiment's achievements are remembered long after battles are over.

## Camouflage

Uniforms are important in battle so that soldiers can tell their friends from their enemies. In the 18th century, when the first modern European armies were formed, uniforms were brightly coloured and easy to recognize; for example, British soldiers wore scarlet (red) coats. However, by the end of the 19th century guns had become much more accurate, which made bright uniforms easy to hit from a long distance away. To make themselves harder to see, soldiers began to wear uniforms that blended into the colours of the countryside. The new camouflage colours, khaki (dull brown), greens and yellows, made it much harder for gunners to shoot at their enemy.

# Sea and Space

When people venture into harsh or alien surroundings, they need clothes to protect them from some very special dangers.

## Extreme cold

One danger is extreme cold, which presents perils for mountaineers climbing above the never-melting snowline on very high mountains, or for explorers in the Arctic or Antarctic, as well as for deep-sea divers. For them, clothing is not only for comfort, it can save their lives. Synthetic materials are a great help because they are very warm yet not bulky, and so allow wearers to move about and do their work more easily.

## Lack of air

An even greater danger in some unfriendly environments is that there is not enough air to breathe. At heights over about 3000 metres above the Earth, the atmosphere becomes thin. So pilots of high-flying military aircraft and climbers on very high mountains wear oxygen masks to help them breathe properly. Climbers also wear special boots with spikes on the soles to stop them from slipping on the steep and icy, rocky mountain surfaces.

Deep-sea divers, some fire officers, and astronauts work where there is no air at all for them to breathe. This is why their suits must include a complete air-supply system.

◀ This skin diver's suit protects her against cold, and supplies her with air. The flippers she wears on her feet help her to swim more powerfully.

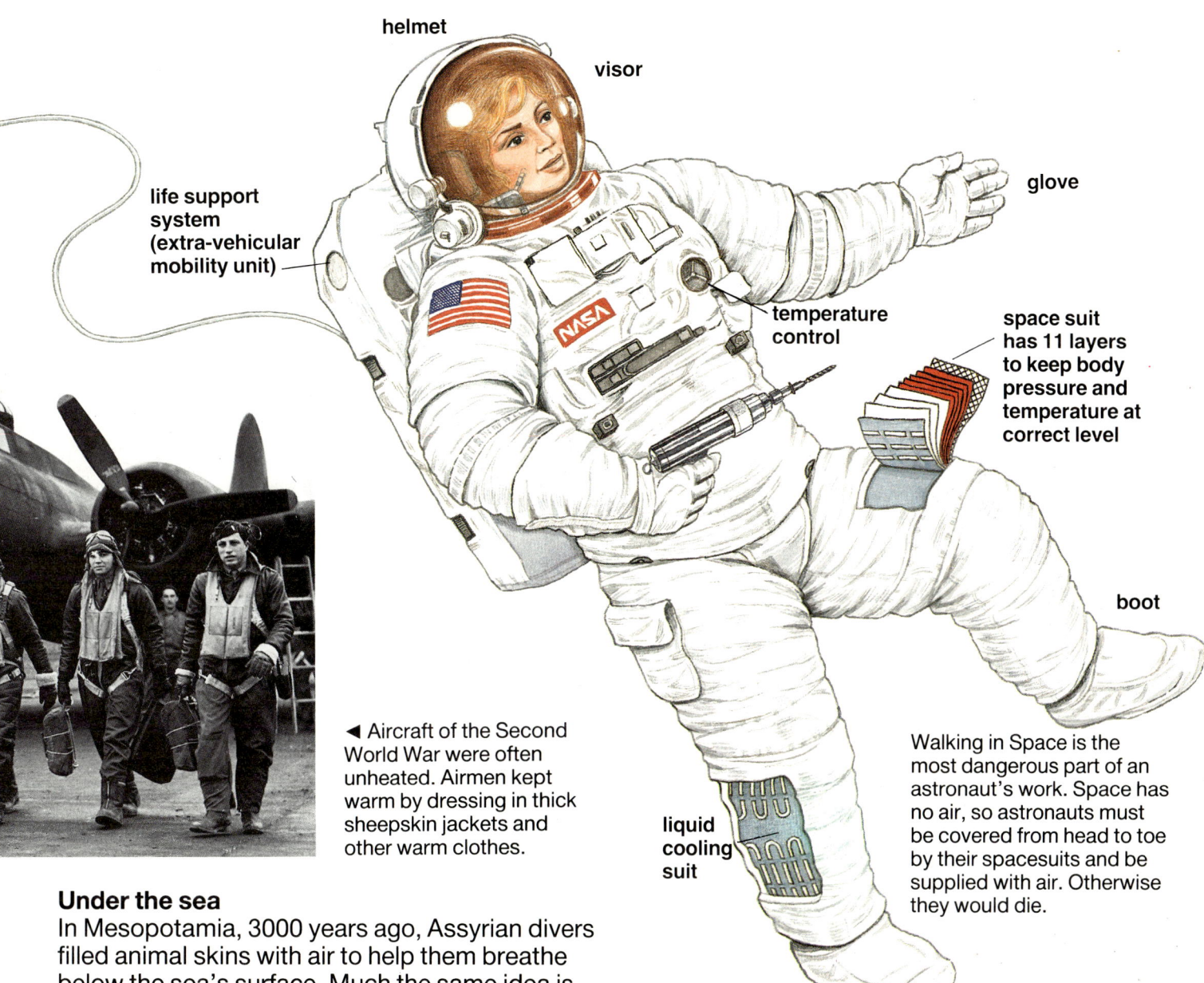

helmet

visor

glove

life support system (extra-vehicular mobility unit)

temperature control

space suit has 11 layers to keep body pressure and temperature at correct level

boot

liquid cooling suit

◄ Aircraft of the Second World War were often unheated. Airmen kept warm by dressing in thick sheepskin jackets and other warm clothes.

Walking in Space is the most dangerous part of an astronaut's work. Space has no air, so astronauts must be covered from head to toe by their spacesuits and be supplied with air. Otherwise they would die.

## Under the sea

In Mesopotamia, 3000 years ago, Assyrian divers filled animal skins with air to help them breathe below the sea's surface. Much the same idea is used today by skin-divers who swim underwater to depths of 90 metres, wearing waterproof 'wet suits', with aqualungs which supply air from cylinders strapped onto their backs.

Much more equipment, though, is needed for deep-sea diving. One of the first pieces of special equipment for this was the helmet invented in 1797 which brought air down to a diver through a tube from the sea's surface. In 1837 a complete 'closed suit' for divers was invented which covered them from head to foot and kept them both dry and supplied with air. However, the deeper a diver goes, the greater the pressure exerted on the diver by the sea. So, for working at very great depths, divers get into a jointed suit with a helmet made of strong metal.

## In space

An astronaut's spacesuit is even more complex. Astronauts wear them when working outside their spacecraft. The latest shuttle suits have their own life-support system attached to the back. Although space is incredibly cold, with temperatures as low as minus 270°C, the sun is always shining and the astronauts can sweat a lot. So astronauts wear liquid cooling suits to keep their body heat at a comfortable level. Over the cooling suit, they wear pressure suits which keep their bodies at a suitable atmospheric pressure. The helmets have microphones so that astronauts can talk with the spacecraft, and gold-plated visors which protect the face from the sun's intense heat and glare.

# Traditional Clothes

A tradition is a practice or custom which has been handed down from one generation to the next. Usually, everyday clothes become traditonal because the need which first gave rise to them has not changed much, if at all. This applies less in the Western world than it does in parts of Asia, Africa and South America, where the way many people live has not altered much for centuries. It also applies to groups of people, like monks or nuns, who continue to follow a religious way of life that has not changed for centuries. Usually, traditional clothes are worn by people whose lives have hardly changed since their ancestors' times.

## In hot climates

Some Australian Aborigines and Amazon tribes in the rainforests of Brazil and Peru still live as their ancestors did thousands of years ago. They still hunt for their food or gather it from the plants around them. They live in extremely hot and sticky climates and so they wear very few clothes, perhaps no more than a loin-cloth, because this is the most practical form of clothing.

These Polish dancers are wearing their traditional folk costume. Folk dress developed from patterns and decorations put on ordinary everyday dress. ▼

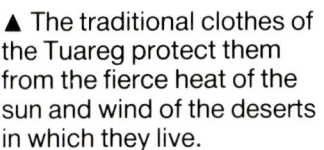

▲ The traditional clothes of the Tuareg protect them from the fierce heat of the sun and wind of the deserts in which they live.

▲ In the Punjab region of eastern India, women wear loose trousers to cover up their legs for reasons of modesty.

▲ Traditional Thai dancers dress in richly-decorated, beautiful clothes to look like the gods they represent in their dance.

## Religious clothes

Christian monks and nuns wear traditional religious clothes to show that they have given their lives to serving God or their fellow human beings. Their plain clothes, habits or robes, show that they have given up the pleasures and rewards of ordinary life.

In Asia Buddhist priests, whose task it is to pray for people, also dress in the humblest way. They wear plain saffron (orange) robes and, as a sign of humility, shave their heads. They own nothing but small bowls with which to beg for their food.

Among Muslims the traditional male headgear, the fez, has also been worn for religious reasons. Muslims and Christians became great rivals after the beginning of Islam, the Muslim religion, in AD 610. This rivalry was especially fierce in

Turkey where, after centuries of war, the Ottoman Turks overthrew the Christian Byzantine Empire in 1453. To show they were *not* Christians, Turks used to wear their own headgear – the fez.

## Muslim women

Traditional dress for Muslim women shows how they are thought of by Islamic people: as being under the care and protection of their men. The protection is so complete that only a woman's husband and family may see her face. So, when women go outside their homes, they must cover their faces. In Morocco, in North Africa, all you can see of some Muslim women is one eye peering through a thin slit in the material covering their heads. In Iran, women traditionally wear the 'chadar', with a face veil called a 'ru-band'. This stretches from eye-level down to the chin and is worn with head-to-toe black robes.

# Entertaining

## Make-believe

Theatre, ballet, opera, pantomime, the circus, and other stage performances are about make-believe. Performers put on make-up and special clothes, their costume, and go out before their audiences to create a small world of fantasy. It may be the fairy-tale world of classical ballet, an opera full of stirring music and splendid singing, or the knockabout antics of circus clowns. Whatever it is, clothes play a very important part.

Clothes can help create a feeling of make-believe. A dream-like impression for ballets can be given by ballerinas dressed in floaty, frilly 'tutus' (short skirts) and delicate bodices and head-dresses. In the circus, though, clowns must be dressed up to look funny. So, they wear crazy-looking hats, baggy trousers, oddly coloured coats and funny footwear. They also put on thick, bright make-up, which makes their eyes and mouths look extra large, and big red noses.

## Theatre

Performers dress up in historical clothes when acting in plays, films or television dramas set in the past. These clothes can be obtained from theatrical costumiers. They can supply Greek chitons, Roman togas, Roman military uniforms, or costumes made in the style of any time up to the present day. In fact, a theatrical costumiers' shop looks very much like a display of clothes and styles worn by people from all over the world during the past 2000 years or so.

Performers acting in plays like those of William Shakespeare (1564-1616) usually wear the costume of the playwright's lifetime. This is known as 'period' costume.

Costumes can be used for special dramatic effect. For instance, at the start of 'Cinderella', the poor, ill-treated young 'Cinders' wears rags. Later, when the Prince has fallen in love with her, 'Cinders' appears dressed like a Princess.

Pantomime performers dress up in bright, fanciful costumes which go with the 'knock-about' fun of this traditional Christmas entertainment on stage.

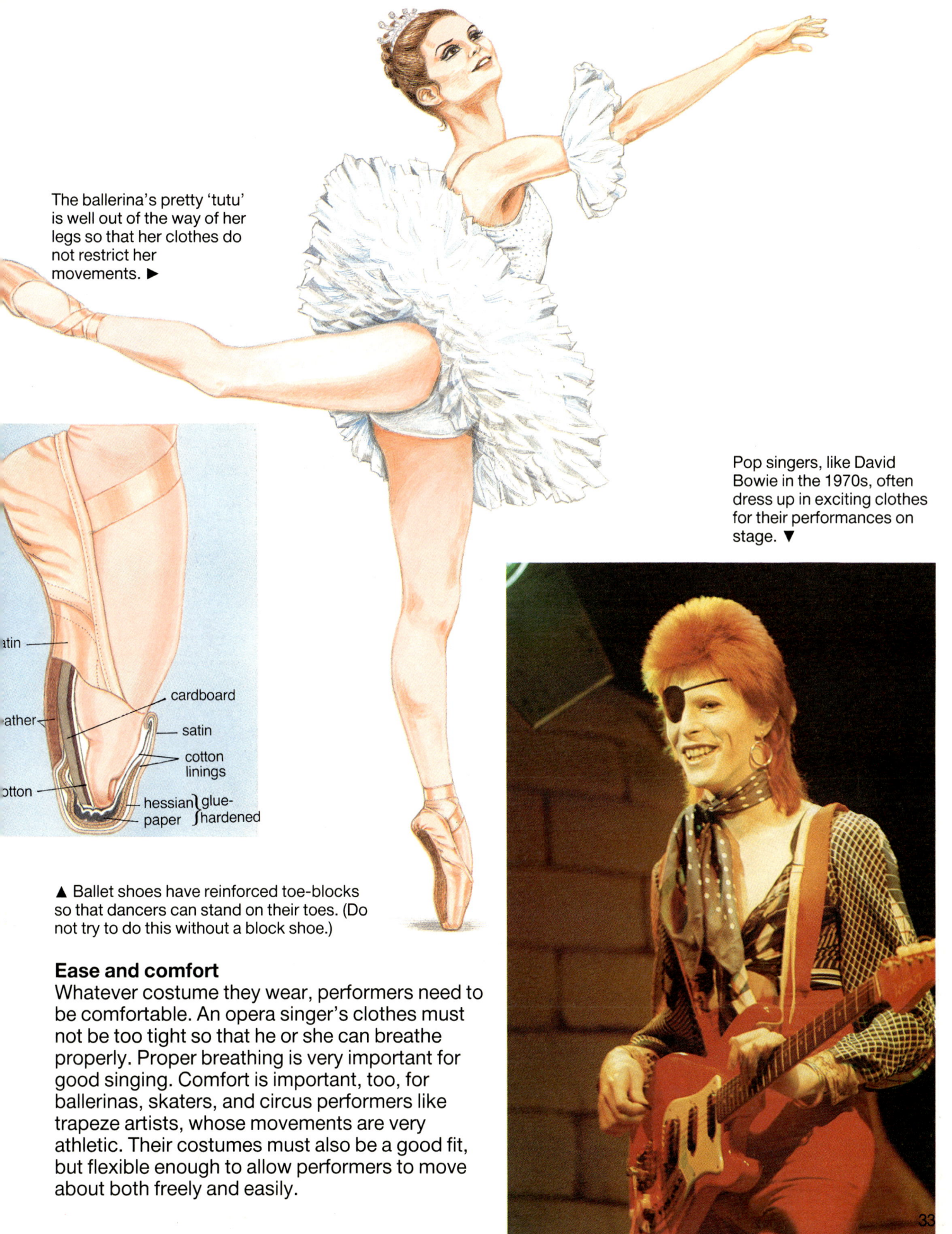

The ballerina's pretty 'tutu' is well out of the way of her legs so that her clothes do not restrict her movements. ▶

satin

cardboard

leather

satin

cotton linings

cotton

hessian } glue-
paper } hardened

▲ Ballet shoes have reinforced toe-blocks so that dancers can stand on their toes. (Do not try to do this without a block shoe.)

Pop singers, like David Bowie in the 1970s, often dress up in exciting clothes for their performances on stage. ▼

## Ease and comfort

Whatever costume they wear, performers need to be comfortable. An opera singer's clothes must not be too tight so that he or she can breathe properly. Proper breathing is very important for good singing. Comfort is important, too, for ballerinas, skaters, and circus performers like trapeze artists, whose movements are very athletic. Their costumes must also be a good fit, but flexible enough to allow performers to move about both freely and easily.

# Sport

Sports people are always testing their energy, strength, skill and speed. Special clothes can help them perform well. Footballers, for instance, would slip and fall more often without their special studded boots. Sports people also need protection. Boxers wear special padded gloves to prevent serious injury to themselves and their opponents. In fast-moving sports like motor-racing or cycling, people need protection against crashes, collisions and fire risks. So, they wear crash-helmets and flame-proof clothes.

In much the same way, ball games can hold many dangers for players. A player might be hit and injured by the ball or by another player's stick or bat. Ice-hockey players dress up in plenty of thick body-padding. This protects them if they bump into other players or fall down on the ice.

Male vaulters wear long trousers for elegance. The trousers need to be close-fitting and able to stretch. ▼

Gymnasts must wear the minimum of clothes to give them complete freedom of movement.▼

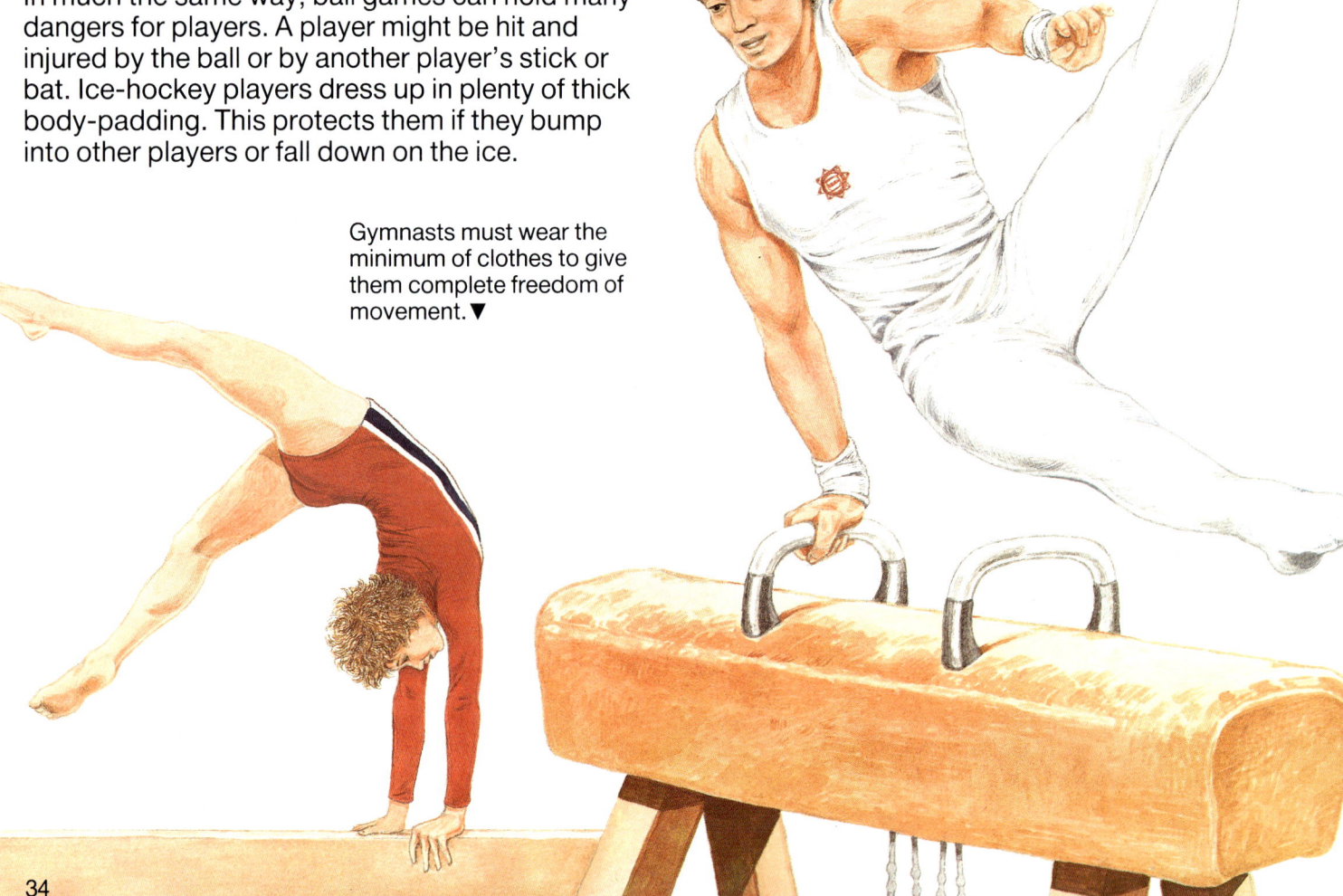

34

Skiers dress to protect themselves against the cold and from falls, but their suits also need to be light and slim-fitting for speed and agility.

## Keeping warm

Being cold can affect sports players in important ways. Their muscles can become strained and injured if not kept properly warm. This is why cricketers often wear pullovers at the start of matches, removing them when they have warmed up. For the same reason, tennis players sometimes begin matches wearing leg-warmers or jumpers.

People who ski must take precautions against cold, for unless the temperature is cold enough, there will be no snow for them to ski on. As a result, skiers can be unrecognizable as individuals as they swoop down the ski slopes, for they cover up from head to toe in warm headgear, gloves and a water-proof ski-suit, as well as goggles to protect their eyes from wind and the white glare of the glistening snow.

## Clothes for speed

Speed is very important to skiers, swimmers, runners and other athletes, so the idea is to dress suitably, but not in bulky clothing: a smoother, slimmer figure produces less 'drag' against the air, an effect which can slow down sportspeople and spoil their performance.

Lighter, less cumbersome clothing helps people to be more agile. In tennis, the modern shorts and tee-shirts, or short-skirted dress for women help explain why the game has become a much faster and more powerful game than it was sixty years ago. Then, men played in long trousers, and women in long skirts reaching down to their knees or even their ankles!

Cricket balls are hard and may be bowled at high speeds. Nowadays, cricketers wear a number of special items for protection. ▼

padded glove

helmet

visor

arm band

thigh pad

shin pad

batting boots

# WHAT IS FASHION?

Fashion in clothes is the wearing of certain styles which are thought to be the smartest and most up-to-date. Until clothes could be made quickly and more cheaply, only wealthy people had enough money to buy the latest fashions and styles. Today, mass-production of inexpensive clothes in factories means that anyone can afford to be fashionable, and ordinary clothing shops can be full of the latest styles.

Fashion styles for women can change very rapidly: what is fashionable to wear in the spring can be out of date by the autumn of the same year. Men's fashions do not change quite so quickly. When they do, they change in small, but distinctive ways. Whereas a new women's fashion can mean a total change in style, a new fashion for men can be nothing more than slightly wider trousers or a longer jacket.

Even so, dressing fashionably appeals to many natural instincts in both men and women. One is the wish not to be out of step with other people. If a man, for example, wears a wide tie when the fashion is for narrower ones, he could feel rather out of place. Television, films, newspapers and magazines can also influence fashion: clothes worn by pop stars, film stars, royalty or politicians are seen by millions of people. These popular personalities have many admirers. Some of them may, for instance, try to copy a favourite pop star by wearing similar clothes.

Models wearing the latest designs at a Paris fashion show. The high cost of these colourful styles puts them beyond the reach of most people. ▶

◀ The high street shops display their own popular fashions that can be afforded and worn by a great number of people.

# Fashion Makers

Until our own century, those who set fashion were usually important or wealthy people.

## Fashion and poor people
Poor people, and that meant most people, did not have the time, the chance or the money to follow fashion. It was more important for them to work, earn money and so feed and house themselves and their families. Even so, after about 1800, some country people adopted their own styles – the brightly decorated clothes we call 'peasant' or 'folk' costume. Both the styles and patterns came from the traditional arts and decorations in countries in Europe.

## Royal fashions
Rich people, however, took their fashions from clothes worn by important persons, such as their kings. For instance, Louis XIV, King of France from 1643 to 1715, wore shoes with wide, stubby heels. Louis's courtiers copied his shoes, and the heels, known as 'Louis heels', are still worn today. Another king, Edward VII of England (1901-1910) was rather fat. To be more comfortable, he undid the bottom button on his waistcoat. This began a fashion among men for leaving the last button on their waistcoat undone.

## Fashion and events
Historical events have also influenced fashion. For instance, clothes became very plain and dull during the strict rule of the Puritans in England (1648-1660). Puritans thought that extravagant and showy clothes were sinful and vain. When the Puritan rule ended, people were glad to be able to wear fancy, colourful clothes again. However, by the time of the Industrial Revolution, after the late 18th century, life in the new factories made these fussy-looking and impractical clothes look out of place and dangerous to work in.

The famous dandy and leader of fashion, George Bryan (Beau) Brummell (1778-1840) spent most of his time and money on his clothes. Whatever he wore was considered good taste. ▶

◀ The style of this French courtier's fussy dress influenced fashion for many years, until Brummell introduced his new style.

◄ Today, the Princess of Wales continues the role of past royal ladies as a 'Queen of Fashion'.

In the Second World War, women's fashions reflected military uniform styles, and shortages of materials led to a plain, neat style known as the 'Utility look'. ▼

## Beau Brummell, the dandy

When factory owners and managers began to wear more practical suits, these suits soon became fashionable among other people. The man who wore the smartest, most beautifully made plain suits was George Bryan 'Beau' Brummell. For a dandy like him, clothes were the most important things in life. Brummell was a close friend, for a time, of the Prince of Wales, the heir to the English throne. After 1799, Brummell's elegant suits and neckties influenced the Prince and other dandies, who put away their frilly clothes and began to dress plainly, like Brummell.

## The Second World War and the New Look

During the Second World War (1939-1945) many men and women joined the armed services and wore uniforms. Fashion tended to reflect this, and women's clothes became very plain, like the Utility outfits in the picture. Also, clothes rationing meant there was not enough cloth for full skirts or frilly decorations. After the war, the famous French designer, Christian Dior, created his 'New Look', which had very full, long skirts and curvy, feminine dresses. The New Look seemed to express the joy and freedom that came with the end of war and great hardship.

# Modern Fashion

Fashion today is made in just the same ways as fashion was made in the past. Important people or events still have a strong influence. For instance, modern space travel and the suits worn by astronauts have influenced fashion ideas. One of them is the fashion for 'moon boots'. These are warm, thick boots, which are worn by both men and women. 'Moon boots' were copied from the boots worn by astronauts when they travelled to the moon and walked on its rough, stony and very cold surface.

## Costly fashion

Some fashionable clothes are still only for those who are rich enough to buy them. In France and Italy, particularly, famous fashion designers display their new styles to their wealthy

customers at fashion shows. The important thing for these customers is to wear clothes by their favourite designer. So, a designer's name can be just as fashionable as the clothes he or she produced. Having that designer's label inside clothes is important to fashionable customers.

## Fashion for everyone

There is, however, another kind of fashion which is important today. This is popular, or 'high street', fashion. This means clothes which are sold in shops in the main or high streets of towns. At one time, many people wanted to wear clothes which were copies of the newest French or Italian fashions. So the high street shops sold copies which were much cheaper to buy than the original clothes. Nowadays, popular styles bear little or no

To us, fashions of the past, like these 18th-century clothes, make children look overdressed. ▼

Today, most children dress in the comfortable casual clothes sold in the high street shops. ▼

◀ In the 1960s many new shops began to sell fashionable clothes for young people. This girl could choose from a wide range of mini-skirted dresses.

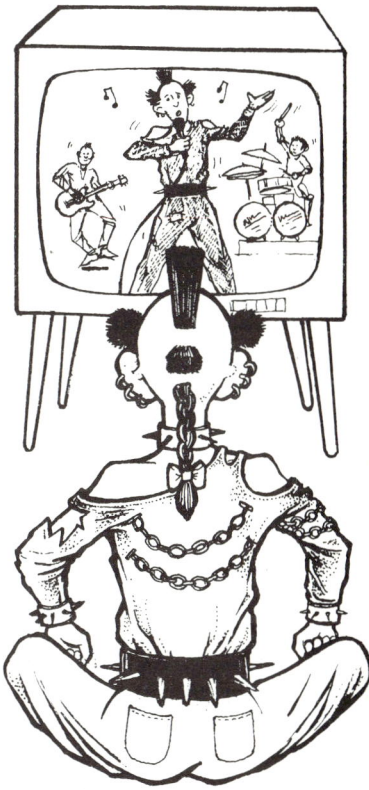

▲ Many new fashions are copied from the clothes seen on television.

relation to the extravagant clothes of designers shown at fashion shows. High street fashions are usually much more plain and ordinary, suitable for everyday wearing. And, because the clothes are mass-produced, they have to be designed to suit everyone, whether they are fat or thin, tall or short.

## Fashion for young people

Special fashions for young people is quite a new idea. After the Second World War wages rose and young people had more money to spend than ever before. 'Teenagers', as they became known, often rebelled against their elders, and one way to show their rebellion was to wear clothes that shocked older people. In Britain, for example, 'Teddy boys' in the 1950s wore long jackets, with

tight trousers and thick-soled shoes. By the 1960s teenage fashions became even more popular; men wore long hair, while women wore daringly short 'mini-skirts' showing much of their legs. Clothes for both sexes were made in all sorts of dazzling colours.

## Punk fashions

Later, in the 1970s, came 'punk' fashions, which started with pop groups. Young people who followed punk fashion painted their faces or dyed their hair in strange, dramatic colours. They also wore clothes that looked deliberately torn, tattered and even dirty. Punk fashions, which made the wearers look even less like their elders than before, remain popular in the 1980s.

# Books and Places

## Books To Read

**Clothes,** Camera as Witness series, Macdonald, 1986.

**Folk Costumes of the World,** Phyllida Legg, Blandford Press Colour series, 1982.

**Dressed for the Job,** Christopher Williams-Mitchell, Blandford Press, 1982.

**Occupational Costume,** Avril Lansdell, Shire, 1977. For pictures of clothes around the world, selected titles from the following series published by Macdonald; 'Looking at Lands'; 'Countries'; 'Religions of the World'.

**Costume Reference Library,** Marion Sichel, Batsford Brothers. This series contains several books, including 'Roman Britain and the Middle Ages'; 'The Eighteenth Century'; 'The Victorians' (that is the 19th century); 'Costume 1918-1939'; '1939-1950'; '1950 to the Present Day'. There are also special subject books in this series, such as 'History of Men's Costume'; 'History of Children's Costume'; 'History of Women's Costume'; and 'Costumes of the Classical World'.

**Four Hundred Years of Fashion,** Victoria and Albert Museum, William Collins, 1984.

**The Anatomy of Costume,** Robert Selbie, Bell & Hyman, 1982.

## Places to visit

In London, there are three important museums where clothes and costumes of different times are shown among the many other exhibits. They are: The Museum of Mankind, 6 Burlington Gardens, London W1X 2EZ. The Science Museum, Exhibition Road, South Kensington, London SW7. The Victoria and Albert Museum, Cromwell Road, South Kensington, London SW7 2RL.

Many other cities and towns in Great Britain have museums which are interesting for visitors who want to see clothes and costumes. Some are costume museums only, others have costumes and clothes as part of their display. These museums are listed in **Museums and Galleries in Great Britain and Northern Ireland,** published by ABC Historic Publications, World Timetable Centre, Church Street, Dunstable, Beds. LU5 4HB. This book is published once a year and lists over one thousand museums and galleries. They include the following:
**Bath:** Museum of Costume (this museum contains costumes from the 17th century to the present).
**Bethnal Green** (London): Museum of Childhood (shows children's costumes and wedding dresses).

# Clothes Search

You can learn quite a lot about the way people dressed in the past by looking at old photographs. Your grandparents may have photographs which will show you what people wore some years ago and how different they are from today's clothes. They may even have some photographs of their own grandparents in the 19th century, like this one which shows a Victorian woman during the 1860s. ▶

**Bexhill:** Manor Costume Museum (a general costume museum covering many periods in costume history).
**Doncaster:** Cusworth Hall Museum (folk-life and folk costume exhibits from the South Yorkshire area).
**Edinburgh:** Canongate Tolbooth (contains models of dress and clan tartans from the Highlands of Scotland).
**King's Lynn:** Museum of Social History (contains displays of home life and everyday dress).
**Leicester:** Museum of Costume, Wygston's House (reconstructions of draper's, milliner's (hatmakers) and cobbler's shops as they were in the 1920s).
**Lincoln:** Museum of Lincolnshire Life (clothes and costumes are included in displays which show the lifestyles and work of Lincolnshire during the last two centuries).
**Manchester:** Gallery of English Costume (contains clothes and fashions from the 17th century to the present day).
**Nottingham:** Museum of Costume and Textiles (costume and costume embroideries of the 17th century; late 18th – mid-20th century costume; underwear 1750-1950).
**Southampton:** Tudor House Museum. A 16th-century mansion, exhibiting costume and local life.
**Totnes:** Devonshire Collection of costume from the last 300 years.
**York:** The Castle Museum (contains displays of clothes of the last 300 years).

◄ You can see how people dressed in the more distant past by looking at church statues or making brass-rubbings of grave brasses that are sometimes found in old churches. Statues were usually made for famous people or those who did important work in the area. As you can see from this picture of a brass-rubbing, these brasses can be very life-like, and you can study many costume details.

◄ Many countries of the world issue postage stamps which show the clothes and costumes people wear today or have worn in the past. These stamps are called 'thematic' stamps. Some countries, like Spain and Greece, have issued stamps showing folk or national costume. You can ask to see costume stamps in stamp shops or at stamp fairs: many are very cheap.

Antique and foreign dolls and porcelain or china figures, like the one in the picture, can give a good 'all-round' view of different costumes. If you have an antique shop in your town, you may be able to see some of these in the window. You can also see them in some museums. The porcelain figures on the right, made in 1752, show the sort of clothes worn by country people. ►

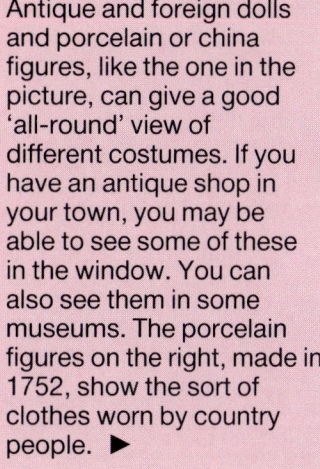

Paintings and tapestries, which you can see in art galleries and museums or in library books about art, can tell you about the way different people dressed and the colours of their clothes. Many great portrait artists working between the 15th and 20th centuries did realistic paintings of clothes. This painting shows the bright colours of suits worn by wealthy men in the 18th century. ►

## Clothes survey

What are men, women and children in your town wearing? It could be fun to find out by doing your own fashion and clothes survey. The first thing to do, though, is to put the people you see into different age groups: for example, up to age 15, up to age 30, up to age 45, and over 45. Of course you can't go up to people and ask how old they are, but do your best to guess their ages. Your first survey could see how many women and girls are wearing trousers, and how many are wearing skirts. Put a tick next to trousers or skirts under the wearer's age group.

You can also do surveys for women and girls who are wearing high heels or low heels on their shoes, or for men who are wearing suits and shirts and ties, and those wearing more casual clothes. If you do your survey with a friend, you can do more complicated surveys together. For example, both of you can do surveys on the hats people wear, but one of you notes the uniform hats (traffic wardens, police, school children, ambulance drivers, railway workers, and so on) and the other notes hats which are worn for protection or decoration. Remember, though, to use your age groups for each person you see.

| Survey | Women in trousers | | Month | March | |
|---|---|---|---|---|---|
| Age group | 0-15 | 15-30 | 30-45 | Over 45 | |
| Quantity seen | ✓✓ | ✓✓✓✓✓ ✓✓✓✓✓ ✓✓✓✓✓ ✓✓✓ | ✓✓✓ ✓✓ | ✓ | |
| TOTALS | 2 | 18 | 5 | 1 | 26 |

| Survey | Hats | | Month | March | |
|---|---|---|---|---|---|
| Age group | 0-15 | 15-30 | 30-45 | Over 45 | |
| Hats as a uniform | ✓✓✓ | ✓✓ | ✓✓✓✓ | ✓✓✓ | |
| TOTALS | 3 | 2 | 4 | 3 | 12 |
| Hats for pleasure or protection | ✓✓ | ✓✓✓ | ✓✓✓ ✓✓ | ✓✓✓✓ ✓✓✓ | |
| TOTALS | 2 | 3 | 5 | 7 | 17 |

# Word List

**Apron** A piece of cloth tied at the back of the neck and waist worn for protection.

**Bloomers** Breeches with wide legs, worn by women cyclists in the 1880s and after.

**Body-padding** Thick pads worn over parts of the body for protection. Often used in the more dangerous sports, like ice-hockey.

**Bustle** Small dome-shaped frame worn below the waist to make women's dresses stick out at the back. A fashion worn during the late 19th century.

**Cloak** Loose outer garment worn over the shoulders.

**Corset** Until the 20th century this was a garment worn under a dress to shape a woman's figure. It was strengthened with whalebone or metal strips.

**Cotton** Fibre of the cotton plant; also used to describe the cloth made from the fibre.

**Crinoline** A set of 12 or more stiff petticoats or a hooped frame worn under a wide-skirted dress. A fashion of the mid-19th century.

**Dandy** In the 18th and 19th centuries, a man to whom clothes and fashion were of the greatest importance.

**Distaff** A stick about one metre long for winding wool or flax: used for spinning cloth.

**Draped clothes** Clothes which hang loosely or in folds about the figure.

**Farthingale** A petticoat with hoops at hip level worn under a dress to make the skirt wide. The wide skirt made the waist look very small. A fashion of the late 16th century.

**Fashion** The newest style in clothes. Also used to describe the newest style in accessories, such as shoes or hats.

**Flax** A plant with a blue flower which is grown for its fibre. The fibre is used to make linen.

**Gaiters** Covering made of cloth or leather, worn from below the knee, or only on the ankles.

**Habit** A long, plain robe worn by monks and nuns.

**Hose** Very close-fitting leg-coverings worn by men in the 13th-16th century. The word is sometimes used today to describe tights or stockings worn by women.

**Linen** Strong, sometimes thick, material made from the fibre of flax. It has been in use since Egyptian times.

**Loom** A machine used for weaving thread into cloth.

**Needle** A narrow pointed piece of metal with an 'eye' at one end in which thread is looped. Used for sewing cloth together.

**Polyester** A synthetic material. Combined with cotton, a natural fibre, polyester makes 'poly-cotton', which is used for shirts and dresses.

**Poncho** A short cloak made of wool. Worn in Peru, Bolivia, Mexico and other parts of Central and South America.

**Sari** Loose-draped robe worn by many women in India and Sri Lanka.

**Sarong** Long draped skirt worn by both men and women in Thailand, Malaysia and other parts of Southeast Asia.

**Shaped clothes** Clothes which are cut and sewn so that they are shaped and fit close to the body.

**Silk** Beautiful, shiny material made from the cocoons of silkworm larvae. It was first made in Asia.

**Spinneret** The hole through which a silkworm spins its thread. Viscose-rayon is spun through a mechanical spinneret which has many extremely fine holes.

**Sumptuary laws** Laws which prevented poor people from wearing fine clothes, owning costly possessions, and eating rich food. In Europe, there were many sumptuary laws before the 18th century.

**Synthetic materials** Artificial materials made from chemical mixtures, such as nylon, polyester and acrylic.

**Thread** Very thin fibre formed from cotton, silk, flax or wool. Used for sewing.

**Toga** Draped robe worn in Ancient Rome by rich and important men and women. Togas reached to the ankles.

**Tunic** Robe worn loose or shaped. They are very simple garments and have been worn from ancient times to the present day.

**Tutu** Frilly, very short skirt worn by ballerinas (female dancers) in classical, or traditional, ballets. They are made from stiff net material.

**Waistcoat** Sleeveless vest with buttons down the front, sometimes worn by men underneath their suit jackets. A three-piece suit consists of jacket, trousers and matching waistcoat. As its name shows, a waistcoat reaches the waist.

# Index